Bedtime Stories for Cats

Other Books by Leigh Anne Jasheway

Bedtime Stories for Dogs

Give Me a Break: For Women Who Have Too Much to Do!

The Rules for Dogs: The Secret to Getting Free Treats for Life

The Rules for Cats: The Secret to Getting Free Catnip for Life

Bedtime Stories for Cats

Leigh Anne Jasheway

Andrews and McMeel
A Universal Press Syndicate Company
Kansas City

Library of Congress Cataloging-in-Publication Data
Jasheway, Leigh Anne.
    Bedtime stories for cats / by Leigh Anne Jasheway.
      p.   cm.
    ISBN 0-8362-2712-3 (hc ; alk. paper)
    1. Cats—Humor.   2. Fairy tales—Humor.   I. Title.
PN6231.C23J37   1997
813'.54—dc21   96–49029
                                                                        CIP

Book design and composition by Top Dog Design.
Click art © T/Maker.

    00 01 QWF 10 9 8 7 6 5

──────── **ATTENTION: SCHOOLS AND BUSINESSES** ────────

Andrews and McMeel books are available at quantity discounts with bulk purchase for educational, business, or sales promotional use. For information, please write to: Special Sales Department, Andrews and McMeel, 4520 Main Street, Kansas City, Missouri 64111.

Contents

Introduction

As the proud parent of one or more cats, you know that your little ones sometimes have difficulty falling asleep—especially if they've had a hard day snoozing in your favorite chair.

When your cat has trouble getting to sleep, you have trouble getting to sleep. And one of you has to get up early in the morning in order to keep your job and keep the other one in cat chow and kitty litter.

Unfortunately, as you may have already discovered, most cats abhor lullabies. They usually give you that look that asks, "Are you out of your mind?" Then they whack you across the nose with one of their paws.

But don't despair, because now there is a way to help get your little ones to settle down for the night without suffering bodily harm: *Bedtime Stories for Cats*. These stories were written specifically with cats like yours in mind. Although, as your cat will surely

 1

remind you, there are no cats like yours.

But most cats do have a few things in common when it comes to stories. For example, they:

- Prefer things short and simple (their lives are complicated enough)
- Like happy endings
- Need really clever stories to challenge their advanced intelligence
- Have excellent senses of humor, although they will deny it if you ask them
- Hate it when people patronize them
- Want everything on their own terms
- Love catnip

Well, except for the catnip, I have tried to make sure that *Bedtime Stories for Cats* meets these criteria. (Blame my editor for leaving out the catnip; she said it made her sneeze.)

Bedtime Stories for Cats is for you if:

- Your cat sleeps on your face
- Your cat drinks the milk out of your cereal bowl while you're still eating

- You only get to read half of what's in the newspaper because your cat always lies right on top of it
- The only one in your house with a diamond necklace is . . . you guessed it
- You've given up on shoes with laces
- You think it's rude when your guests exclaim, "There's cat hair in the pasta!"
- You haven't been to the dentist for fourteen years, but your cat went last week
- You have a special shelf in the bathroom for kitty toiletries (shampoo, toothpaste, bath oil, whisker wax . . .)

Each of the stories in this book was cat-tested by a panel of felines—Bootsy, Spooky, Roxxy, Coco, and Big Dan. No story made it in the book unless it received five cat paws up.

So snuggle up with your little angel and read on. You'll both fall asleep faster and dream pleasant dreams.

Rumpled Katzkin

There once was a computer programmer named Howie Katzkin who lived in a huge penthouse apartment with a beautiful Siamese cat whom he called Phoebe, although she preferred Babs.

Howie was very good at his job, and he spent almost all his time at work—even the weekends. This meant that Phoebe/Babs had that big apartment all to herself. And although she was a proud and independent cat, just once in a while Phoebe wished someone

 5

would rub her ears or stroke her belly—or at least notice that she had shredded yet another set of drapes.

Of course, she couldn't very well just come out and say so. It was in the Cat Rule Book: "Rule #42: Never beg for attention. Only dogs do that."

Days passed, and weeks and months and years. Phoebe had a lot of time on her paws, so she prowled, she roamed, and she watched infomercials. She even took correspondence courses from Feline University. She had degrees in architecture and art, as well as a certificate in auto repair (she was working her way through the courses alphabetically). Next on the list—belly dancing.

Yes, Phoebe was one talented cat. Unfortunately, no one was ever around to see just how talented she was.

One day, Howie got beeped at the office. He dialed the number, and the voice at the other end of the phone said, "King of Late Night Comedy's office, court jester speaking." As it turned out, the king had a computer virus (perhaps he forgot to wash his hands before he booted up the hard drive). And when it came to getting rid of computer bugs, Howie was the man. Everyone knew that.

Howie went straight from work over to the king's studio. He didn't even stop by the apartment to check on Phoebe. It wasn't that he was a bad man; it was just that he was unthinking and insensitive to her needs. Maybe if Phoebe had had computer problems of her own . . . but of course, she hadn't made it to the computer classes at Feline University yet.

Anyway, as Howie worked on the computer, the king stood nearby and cracked jokes.

Howie, not knowing any jokes of his own and trying not to appear too dull and nerdlike, tried to think of something interesting to say. Finally, the pressure got to be too much, and he just blurted out, "I have a cat who can impersonate Barbra Streisand."

You see, sometimes late at night when Howie would drag himself home from work, he would hear the unmistakable sounds of Ms. Streisand coming from Phoebe's closet. Now, it is true that it could have just been Phoebe playing her portable CD player, but he thought not.

"Wow," exclaimed the king. "If your cat is as talented as you say, I guarantee I can make her a star. Bring her by the studio tomorrow morning."

By the time Howie finally got home, it was late. He looked all around the apartment and couldn't find Phoebe anywhere. And there was no music coming from the closet. So he went right to bed.

He couldn't find Phoebe because she was hiding under the bed. She had waited up until midnight hoping that he would get home so they could at least say good night. No such luck. Needless to say, Phoebe was miffed. While Howie was sleeping, she left a nice big hair ball on his pillow.

The next morning, Howie awoke at 7:00 A.M. He saw the hair ball on his pillow, thought it was a spider, and jumped straight up in the air. Phoebe chuckled. (If you don't think cats chuckle, you haven't been paying attention.)

Later that morning, while Phoebe was napping, Howie got out her carrier and put her in it. This really ticked Phoebe off. Okay, so she had an attitude problem. But she had rights.

She was mad because she had been dreaming that she had won the Cat Fancy Publishers Clearinghouse Sweepstakes and was waiting for a dump truck to deliver her lifetime supply of catnip. And she was mad about the carrier. She hated that carrier. After all, it was, and she could hardly bring herself to say the word, *plastic*.

Howie and Phoebe arrived at the king's studio at ten-ish. That's actually what the clock said—"ten-ish." After all, this was show business.

The king greeted them and showed them to the greenroom. "Better warm up those vocal chords," he advised Phoebe as he headed off to makeup.

Howie opened Phoebe's carrier, and she shot out like the cork from a bottle of champagne. She landed right on top of a fine leather couch. "What," she hissed, "is this all about? And let me remind you that I still have all my claws and that this couch looks like it would give me a really nice manicure."

Howie explained sheepishly about the king and Barbra Streisand. "So, can you do Barbra, or should I go apologize?" Howie asked timidly.

"Maybe I can, and maybe I can't," replied Phoebe teasingly. "What will you give me if I do?" Phoebe was hoping he'd take a day off and toss around a ball of aluminum foil with her—or something.

"I'll give you my watch," Howie said. This was not what Phoebe had in mind.

She took the watch anyway and looked at it. It was a really nice watch—gold and silver and no plastic. Howie may have been a nerd, but he was a well-paid nerd. She slipped it on over her head. It made an elegant collar. She looked in the mirror.

"People. People who need people," Phoebe sang, sounding just like Barbra Streisand.

Howie jumped up ecstatically. "You can sing like Barbra. That's amazing."

"Yes, I can sing. I can also do many other amazing things, which you would know if you ever spent any time with me," Phoebe said cattily.

"We're going to be rich," Howie continued. "Or, richer . . ."

"What do you mean, 'We'?" Phoebe queried, eyeing him with her piercing green-eyed stare. "I think I need more motivation. What else can you give me?"

While she waited, Phoebe jumped up on the table that was covered with snacks for the

King of Late Night Comedy's guests. She
snagged a goldfish from a bowl. "Yuck!" she
yowled. "This doesn't taste fishy."

Howie watched her prowl around the table
looking for edibles and said, "How about if I
give you my gold ring?"

Howie may have been a genius of a computer programmer, but when it came to picking up on hints, he was an idiot.

Phoebe took the ring and slipped it onto
her forepaw. It made a nice bracelet and was
fitting for a cat of her great beauty. ". . . are the
luckiest people in the world." Phoebe belted
out one more line of her best Barbra Streisand
song.

Howie grinned and straightened his tie. He
looked kind of cute all dressed up, thought
Phoebe—except for those dorky white socks

he always wore even though she shredded every pair he brought into the house. He must have kept a stockpile of them at work.

"You know," Phoebe lamented, "being a star can be very stressful. I'm going to need some special attention." She thought she'd make her point just a little more clearly. "What can you do to ease my stress?"

Howie stared at the floor. Then he got an idea. "Here, you can have my jacket."

It was a lovely camel hair jacket. Phoebe clawed and dug and made herself a nice nest. Exhausted from dropping clues for the clueless, she settled down to take a nap. "Don't wake me until it's time to go onstage."

Twenty minutes later, a stagehand arrived to tell Phoebe she had two minutes until show time. She woke up and looked at Howie. He looked so sweet and innocent. She decided just to come out with it, rule book or no rule book.

"You know, Howie, I don't need all this stuff. All I want is some love and attention. And not all the time, mind you. Just occasionally. Rub my ears. Scratch my belly. Let me play with your shoelaces. Do you think you can make that kind of commitment?"

Howie looked shocked. He stared at his shoelaces. Then he strained his neck trying to see what time it was by the watch Phoebe was wearing around her neck.

Finally, he turned to her and said, "Okay, I'll do it. What do you say I take a month off and we go to the country? We can run in the fields; you can catch mice. I'll sing you lullabies every night."

Phoebe was ecstatic. This was more of a commitment than she thought he was capable of. "Well, I can do without the lullabies," she purred. "Remember, I've heard you sing in the shower. But as for the rest, you've got a deal."

She gave Howie his watch and ring back—and his very rumpled jacket.

Seconds later, Phoebe and Howie made their television debuts. As Howie walked out onstage, the king took one look at Howie's jacket and introduced him as "Rumpled Katzkin." And since this got a big laugh from the audience, he kept calling him that and the name stuck.

Well, the rest of the story goes like this. That night, Phoebe was a star. But right after that, Phoebe and Howie went to the country on vacation. And in the four weeks they were gone, everyone—the audience, the king, the media—forgot all about them, as often happens.

But it didn't matter one bit because Phoebe had finally gotten what she wanted. And Howie discovered that he actually liked being in a relationship. These days, Howie and Phoebe are actually talking about adopting a kitten.

Kitty and the Beast

A long time ago, or was it yesterday? I really don't remember.

Well, anyway. There once was a rich used-car dealer named Ed who had three daughters. Shannon and Heather, the older daughters, were self-involved, lazy, and thoughtless. They lay around the house all day watching MTV and dreaming up new parts of their bodies to get pierced or tattooed. They took after their mother who had run away two years earlier with an accountant for the circus.

But the youngest daughter, Kitty, was humble, hardworking, and kind—not to mention completely tattoo-free.

One day, Ed lost his dealership because a local news reporter discovered that he had been setting the odometers back on all his used cars. So he had to move his family from their big house in the suburbs to a small apartment in the nearby city.

Shannon and Heather griped constantly about the new place. "It's so ugly here," they'd whine, pointing at the graffiti on the walls all around them. "There's nothing to do," Heather would moan. "We live next door to a fast-food restaurant, for God's sake!" Shannon would say in a snit. Not that it really mattered since all they did was lie around all day watching MTV. . . but we already covered that.

Kitty, on the other hand, studied hard, started making friends, and never, ever complained. She was the kind of daughter that made other daughters look bad.

Ed, meanwhile, had learned his lesson and decided to wise up and get a good, honest job—one where he wouldn't end up with a reporter sticking a microphone in his face and demanding, "Is it true that you're a crook?" Obviously law and politics were out. So he decided to become a cable installer.

As it happened, there was a big cable installer training conference in the biggest city in the state. So Ed decided to go.

When they found out their father was going to be staying at one of the fanciest hotels in the city, Heather and Shannon demanded, "Bring us back those monogrammed bathrobes, and those little shampoos, and some towels. And don't forget those chocolates they leave on your pillow every night."

"What would you like me to bring back, Kitty?" asked Ed.

Kitty said humbly, "I only want your safe return, Father, and a red rose from the flowers they keep in the hotel lobby."

On his way to the big city, Ed got lost. You know how it is with men and cars. They think they know where they're going, and then they get lost, and of course they're not going to stop and ask anyone for directions. But that's a whole other story.

Anyway, when he finally ran out of gas and had to pull over, Ed noticed a house on the side of the road. He knocked on the door and called out, "Is anyone here?"

No one answered, so he went inside. He

was tired from the long drive and noticed a cappuccino maker on the kitchen counter, so he made himself a cup. There wasn't a phone anywhere to be found, and since Ed was still sleepy (turns out it was decaf cappuccino in the machine), he decided to take a short nap on the couch. Before he fell asleep he felt that he was being watched.

When he finally awoke the next morning, he decided to try to find a phone. But on the way out, he noticed a rose garden outside the house. He stopped and picked one for Kitty.

HERE IS ED'S SIDE OF THE STORY:

Suddenly, a very large, very unsightly cat stood before me, hackles raised. "My name is Beast. What do you think you're doing in my garden?" he roared.

I was very frightened. You wouldn't have

believed the size of this thing. It must have weighed a good fifty pounds. Where a tail should have been, there was only a stump. It was the color of dried mud, and its face had a permanent scowl.

I begged the beast for mercy. "Please don't hurt me. I was just picking a rose for my daughter. I didn't mean any harm."

But the hulking creature did not sway. He demanded I take him home with me or he'd shred my new suit and prove that my steel-belted radials were no match for his claws.

HERE IS BEAST'S SIDE OF THE STORY:

I was dozing peacefully in the early morning sun when a large, rude man practically stepped on me. I was lucky I had recently lost all that weight, or he wouldn't have missed me.

I arose as nicely as possible and said, "Excuse me, kind sir. My name is Beast. I would truly appreciate it if you wouldn't pick these roses. I like to lie in their shade and smell their beautiful scent.

Even though I acted calm, inside I was petrified. The man was huge. He must have weighed a good 350 pounds. Where a neck should have been, there was only a stump, and his head seemed to sit right on top of his shoulders. That thing on the top of his head that might have passed for hair among humans resembled the rat I killed the other day under the front porch.

"Outta my way you ugly creature," yelled the man, which I thought was very rude, especially considering he was no beauty-contest winner himself. "I promised my daughter a rose, and she's gonna get one."

Actually, I was moved by the man's concern for his daughter. So I said nicely, "Why don't you take me home to meet your daughter? I'm sure she'd love a companion."

As you know, there are at least two sides to every story, and since we weren't actually there, we'll never know whose version to believe. One way or another, Beast ended up going home with Ed. And there were scratches—both from cat claws and from roses—on both of them.

When Ed got home, his daughters Heather and Shannon practically knocked him over. "What'd you bring us? What'd you bring us?" they shrieked. Suddenly they saw a hideous, overweight cat sitting on the floor.

"That's disgusting! Get it out of here!" they screamed as they tore through their father's luggage looking for goodies.

Meanwhile, Kitty came in from the kitchen

where she had been doing dishes (she really was the perfect child—but, after all, this *is* a fairy tale). She took one look at Beast and thought to herself, "Well, he's kind of odd-looking, but it would be fun to have someone to play with."

"Hello, Father," Kitty said as her sisters ran by her after having just discovered that they were missing *House of Style* on MTV. "And hello to you, too, cat."

"My name is Beast," said the cat as he gazed around the house, trying to find a litter box. After all, it had been a long ride.

"Would you like to go out to play?" asked Kitty.

Beast nodded. "But first, if you'll excuse me, I have to visit a bush."

Days passed. Heather and Shannon ridiculed Beast every time they saw him. They made up names for him. "Tubbo." "Ugkins." "Elephant

Cat." This was really ironic considering the sisters were no great beauties themselves, what with all the tattoos and body piercing—not to mention the fact that they had recently dyed their hair green.

Ed just mostly ignored Beast. He reminded him too much of someone he knew. He wasn't sure who.

Kitty, on the other hand, really liked having Beast around. Every day when she got home from school, they'd play in the yard (it took Kitty a while to get used to the idea of batting half-dead insects around and calling it fun, but she eventually did). Every night she'd comb Beast's fur.

And Beast would always look right at Kitty and ask, "Tell me, Kitty, . . . am I very ugly?"

And because she was way too honest for

her own good, Kitty always said, "Yes, Beast, you are. But I'm fond of you just the same."

One day at school, all the children were told that they could bring their pets to class in one week for a pet parade.

Though she really liked Beast, Kitty could not imagine showing him to her classmates. After all, he was so ugly.

But when she got home, Shannon and Heather met her at the door. "Are you going to take Beast to class?" they giggled. They thought the whole thing was very funny.

"What's this all about?" their father asked.

Shannon said, "All the kids in Kitty's class get to bring in their pets. They're going to have a parade and a beauty contest." At that, Shannon and Heather began to laugh uncontrollably. "Imagine Beast in a beauty contest."

"So," their father asked, "are you going to take Beast to school?"

"No," replied Kitty quietly. "I just can't do it. He's too hideous. Everyone would make fun of him. And everyone would make fun of me too."

Beast, standing under the table out of sight, heard everything and decided to run away.

That night Kitty went to find Beast to comb him. She looked everywhere—all his favorite places—the sofa, the closet, the newspaper recycling bin. He was nowhere to be found.

The days passed, and Beast did not come home. Kitty was very sad. Even her sisters were a little sad. After all, it was fun making fun of that big, fat cat.

And Ed kind of missed him too. It was like a part of him was missing. But he didn't really understand why.

Kitty cried herself to sleep every night.

Pretty soon it was the next week, and when Kitty went to school, all the other girls and boys had their favorite animals with them. There were cats and dogs and ferrets and hamsters and a cockatiel and a snake. And an iguana.

And even though some were better looking than others, it was clear that all of the children loved their pets a lot—even Alfred, the boy with the iguana. He even kissed his iguana on the nose (Kitty thought that was the iguana's nose, but she really couldn't be sure).

And this made Kitty even sadder.

That night, Kitty decided she had to get Beast back. So she made fliers to put up around the neighborhood.

There weren't any pictures of Beast to put on the fliers (after all, no one had wanted to take his picture), so Kitty drew his likeness.

And she made him very beautiful. Under the hand-drawn picture she wrote, "Beast, please come home. I love you. Kitty."

The next morning when she got up, Kitty found Beast sleeping peacefully next to her on her pillow. She jumped for joy and shouted, "Beast, you're back!"

Beast just smiled and looked straight at Kitty and said, "Am I very ugly?"

To which Kitty replied, "Not at all. In fact, you may be the most beautiful creature in the world."

Kitty's sisters continued to tease Beast, but maybe a little less viciously. And you could tell, deep down, under the tattoos and the green hair, they actually seemed a little fond of him.

And Ed, well, he got the job as a cable installer, which put him in a better mood. He even seemed to like Beast most days. Even though he still reminded him of someone.

And the next time the kids were invited to bring their pets to school, Kitty took Beast and showed him off proudly.

Which just goes to show that beauty is more than fur-deep.

The Three Kitty Cats Gruff

Once upon a time there were three kitty cats. One was a little kitty cat, one was a middle-sized kitty cat, and one was so big that she didn't even fit on the scale in the vet's office.

The smallest kitty cat was named Samson, and the medium-sized one was named Delilah. And, through some unfortunate twist of fate, the biggest kitty cat was called Tiny.

Everyone in the village teased Tiny. They called her names and made fun of her rolls of fat. As a result, Tiny had very low self-esteem.

Most of the time she stared at the ground when she walked because she was so embarrassed. And of course, as you know, when you watch the ground as you walk, you tend to be quite klutzy.

The kitty cats all belonged to a family named Gruff, and they were known together as the Kitty Cats Gruff.

One sunny day, the three Kitty Cats Gruff were out in a field lying in the sun. Suddenly Samson said, "Let's go over that bridge and explore." Delilah was all for the idea, but Tiny hesitated.

You see, like many cats Tiny had a sixth sense about things. And right now her sixth sense was telling her that crossing the bridge was dangerous. Besides, Tiny remembered hearing someone once say that "curiosity killed the cat."

So she muttered, "I think we should just stay

here and be happy with what we've got." But because she mumbled her words and stared at the ground, Samson and Delilah started toward the bridge.

Tiny decided to go along too. She didn't like to be alone.

Samson got to the bridge first, and he started to cross. Under the bridge lived a huge, ugly troll with an attitude problem.

The troll's story is this: Up until a few days earlier, he had been a happy plastic doll that belonged to the Gruff children. But somehow, he had turned into a real, living creature. Maybe it was a spell, or maybe it was something he ate. We'll never know. The troll wasn't at all happy about his big plastic belly or his unmanageable green hair. So you can see why he would be in a foul mood most of the time.

Anyway, back to the Kitty Cats Gruff.

Samson started to cross the bridge. He got halfway across the bridge and stood looking out at the water below. Suddenly there was a loud sneeze from under the bridge. Then another. And another.

It was the troll. As it happens, he was allergic to cats. And allergies did nothing to improve his mood.

"Who's that up on the bridge?" he roared. "I'm coming up there to gobble you up!" He just realized how hungry he was. After all, he had that big plastic belly to feed.

"Oh, no. Don't do that," meowed Samson. "I am the littlest Kitty Cat. Wait until my sister comes across the bridge. She's *much* bigger." Samson had absolutely no family loyalty.

"Okay," grumbled the troll. "I'll wait."

Samson crossed the bridge and went up to

explore. Then Delilah started across the bridge, and just when she had gotten halfway, there was loud sneezing from below.

"Not this again!" wheezed the troll, whose eyes were now red and teary. "Who's up on that bridge? I'm going to come gobble you up."

"Do you really want to do that?" asked Delilah. "How do you think eating me will make you feel?" Delilah had been reading some books on psychology she had found in the basement.

The troll responded, "It will make me feel full. And it will stop this blasted allergy attack." So he started up toward the bridge.

Frightened, Delilah meowed, "Why don't you wait just a few minutes? My sister is right behind me and she's *huge*!" Again with the family loyalty. Delilah would probably have sold her grandmother for catnip.

Once again the troll decided to wait. And Delilah went over the hill to explore.

Tiny came to the bridge and hesitated because, you see, Tiny was scared of heights, and the bridge was very high. Besides, she really had no desire to go see what was on the other side.

So she sat down in the field and watched the butterflies instead.

Meanwhile, the troll was feeling really mean and hungry. He finally realized that there was no third Kitty Cat coming by to satisfy his growling stomach. So he decided to go after Samson and Delilah.

He bolted up the hillside and chased down Samson and Delilah, which wasn't very hard at all because what they had found on the other side of the bridge was nothing—no trees, no tall grass, no butterflies, no catnip, no free cat

chow, no mice to chase . . . nothing. So there was nowhere for them to hide.

"You lied to me!" shouted the troll. "You said there was a really big cat coming and that I should wait. Well, I waited, and now I'm good and hungry, and you are the featured menu special."

Samson and Delilah began to cry. Louder and louder. They yelled for Tiny, "Help!"

Tiny looked up from her butterfly watching and saw some kind of commotion on the other side. So, tentatively, she crossed the bridge.

Meanwhile, Samson and Delilah were running as fast as they could. And before you knew it, they were in the river under the bridge. This was a big problem because they couldn't swim.

"Help, we're drowning," they cried to Tiny, who had just reached the other side.

So Tiny dove into the icy water and cat-paddled her way to her siblings. She had very little trouble because all that fat floated. Samson and Delilah climbed aboard, and they floated to the other shore.

"Boy, are we lucky," said Samson. "Yeah, if you hadn't been so fat, we couldn't have floated to safety," said Delilah. Then they both did something they had never done before. They thanked Tiny.

Meanwhile, the troll reconsidered his options. He could cross the bridge and begin the chase again, but he wasn't sure cats would make such a good meal after all. For one thing, they were hairy. And the troll really didn't want to know what it felt like to have a hair ball.

So he changed his mind and decided to have fish instead.

When Samson and Delilah and Tiny got home they were wet and tired. But Tiny walked with her head held high because she was a hero. (And, as she soon discovered, it was a lot easier to watch butterflies that way.)

And even though Tiny had warned her siblings not to cross the bridge, she never, ever said "I told you so." And they never made fun of her weight again.

Puss and the Missing Boots

I was sitting at my desk waiting for the phone call from police headquarters when she walked in. She was tall, blond, and would have been quite beautiful if that type interested me and if her mascara hadn't been smeared down her face like the wreck of the *Exxon Valdez*.

I'm a cat. My type is small and fluffy, with a smile that says, "Your closet or mine?" But I digress. . . .

She plopped herself down on the dumpster next to my desk—this is the low-rent district.

What can I say? Business hasn't been so good lately. Actually, business hasn't been so good ever.

It was then I noticed that she wasn't wearing shoes.

"You've gotta help me," she implored breathlessly. "A cat burglar took my boots."

"Slow down just a minute, lady," I replied in my best detective voice. "Let's back up. The name's Puss, Pussywillow Claudius Rex the Third, to be exact. And you are?"

"Dollface Molloy. Charmed to make your acquaintance." She wiped her eyes with a hankie. A scented hankie. This was one classy broad. (The editors of this book would like to interrupt this paragraph to let the reader know that they do not approve of the word "broad" or even the name "Dollface." However, in the interest of sticking to the detective novel genre, we'll let it pass . . . for now.)

"Dollface," I said. I looked her over. Her stockings had more runs than the New York Yankees. I made a note. "Let me see if I've got this right. A cat burglar took your boots. And you want me to track him down. Does that about cover it?"

"That covers it." She lit a cigarette.

"Hey, put that out," I said forcefully. "This is a nonsmoking detective story. Besides, don't you know that stuff will kill you?"

She shrugged her milky-white shoulders and stubbed out the cigarette. Her shoulders reminded me of that time in Paris when I shared a bowl of milk with that cute little French cat, Oui-Oui. For a moment, I stared off into space, remembering the past. I loosened my cat collar.

But she broke my silence. "Excuse me. My boots? Can you help me or not?"

"Well, you did say it was a cat burglar. And I am a cat detective. I guess I'm the man, uh, cat, for the job." I glanced at my watch. I wanted her to think I had other appointments.

"Oh, good," she sighed with relief. "I love those boots. They're one of a kind—blue suede, over-the-knee. They cost me twelve hundred dollars."

"Twelve hundred dollars, huh? Then I guess you can afford my fee—a case of Friskies, two bags of catnip, and a big ball of yarn. Wool, not acrylic."

"Deal," she said. She reached into her purse and pulled out a rubber mouse. "Here's your retainer."

"Thanks, Dollface." I took the mouse. It was a beaut.

"Here's my address." She handed me a slip of paper. It was barely legible, what with the mascara stains. She stood up, wiped the grime from her dress, and disappeared as quickly as she had appeared.

"I love this job," I thought as she walked out of my alley.

The next morning, I got right to work on the case. I called all the pawn shops. No blue suede, over-the-knee boots had surfaced overnight.

I visited my snitch, Eddie, an American shorthair who'd been in trouble with the law more than once. He clammed up so tight, his whiskers vibrated. No help at all. I'd have to solve this one on my own.

Around 1:30 P.M., after my usual lunch of anchovies and beer, I went to the address on the slip of paper. Nice part of town.

Unfortunately, heartburn kicked in just as I reached her apartment.

I let myself in the dog door. I sniffed the air. No dogs around now.

So I decided to case the joint. Well, actually, I mostly just walked around and sniffed the carpet, but in detective lingo, that's casing the joint.

Someone had obviously done some damage. The place was a mess. There was unfolded laundry on the sofa, green stuff growing in the refrigerator, and pizza boxes under the couch. That Dollface was one sloppy housekeeper. But, boy, did she have good taste in pizza—anchovy and pineapple. I wrapped up a few pieces for a midafternoon snack.

I didn't see any real sign of foul play.

I went into the bedroom. The closet door was open. I peeked inside. Shoes everywhere—

pumps, sneakers, moccasins, slippers, sandals, sling backs, Earth shoes—piled to the ceiling. But no boots. Not one pair of boots to be seen anywhere.

I was just about to leave the scene of the crime when I spotted something on the floor next to the trash can. No, it wasn't a mouse. It was a clue. It was *the* clue.

The next day, she showed up again. This time her mascara was intact, and she was wearing shoes. Red leather boots to be exact. New, from the looks of it.

"So, I see you got some new boots," I offered. "I suppose you used the insurance money to pay for them."

"Yes, what about it?" she replied a little too defensively. "A girl's gotta have boots. Now, what did you find out about the cat burglar?"

I waited a few seconds to build up tension.

Right about this point I was wishing I had a tape player in my office so I could have put on some really suspenseful music to set the mood just right, like in the *Maltese Falcon* or *Columbo* or something.

Finally, I couldn't take it any more. "Well, I know who stole your boots. But I don't think you'll be happy with what I found out."

Dollface leaned forward, her ample cleavage almost spilling from her dress. This did not impress me at all. Although it did make me think of that nice-looking calico I'd gone out with last week. I made a mental note to call her.

"Who did it?" she asked nervously, biting her lip.

"Well, I think you know the answer to that, now don't you?" I walked slowly away from her.

"No, I have no idea. Who did it?"

I whirled back around and stared at her face-to-face. Well, maybe face-to-ankle. "It was you, and you know it."

"That's preposterous!" she huffed. "You're a fraud! Don't expect me to pay you." With that, she turned on the heel of her brand-new boot and started to exit.

"Wait a minute. You might be interested in a little something I picked up at the scene of the crime." I pulled out the slip of paper.

"What's that?" she asked nonchalantly.

"A receipt from Bob's Boot Repair dated two days ago."

"Well, that doesn't prove anything," she stared at me, her eyes darker than a black hole and just as inviting. "I use Bob all the time. For my boot repair, I mean."

I just had to grin. I'm sure I looked like the cat who swallowed the canary. But I had a right to feel smug. "I called Bob this morning. Turns out he's had your boots all along. Fixing the heel, he said. Seems no one stole your boots. My guess is you've just defrauded your insurance company."

Before she could deny anything, the police showed up. Dollface started to cry. Mascara again. Everywhere.

I stretched. And yawned. It had been a long day. I'd missed my sixteen-hour cat nap. Another day, another case solved.

Boy, I love this job. And maybe someday I'll even get paid.

Katpunzel

Once upon a time, a man and his wife were very unhappy because they had no children.

All their friends with children tried to cheer them up by telling them horror stories about getting up twenty times in the middle of the night, changing dirty diapers at the mall, and arriving at work only to find surprise baby goo all over your shirt.

But the stories didn't work. They were still very sad.

So they decided to get a cat. They went to

the animal shelter and picked out a beautiful black cat with eyes the color of emeralds and a tongue pinker than a newborn baby.

They decided to call the cat Katpunzel. This was okay with her. It certainly beat being called Number Seventeen, which was her name at the shelter. Besides, she was pretty sure her name should have been Number One.

Katpunzel went right into the spare bedroom and made herself at home. She unpacked her suitcase and put the pictures of her brothers and sisters on the nightstand. As she sat in the middle of her new queen-sized brass bed grooming herself that first night, Katpunzel thought to herself, "Home at last."

Because the couple had no children, they spoiled Katpunzel. Every time Katpunzel saw something in a magazine or on TV that she wanted, they bought it for her. In a few short months, her once spacious bedroom was getting cramped. There was pearl jewelry from the Home Shopping Network (Katpunzel looked fabulous in pearls), two of those carpeted kitty tree houses from the pet store, and a shiatsu massage chair for days when Katpunzel was feeling a little tense.

And, of course, a Jacuzzi. That took up a lot of room.

Now you might think that cats dislike getting wet, and you'd be right, for the most part. Katpunzel, on the other hand, loved water—especially hot water with jet streams. This is just one of the things that made her much different from other cats you may know.

Now as it happened, Katpunzel and her people lived on the thirty-second floor of a condo in the city that was surrounded on three sides by concrete. But out the window of their living room, they could see a beautiful garden way down below.

Every morning, the wife would look out the window and see an old lady pulling weeds and planting flowers and just making things grow beautifully. Katpunzel, on the other hand, spent her mornings in the Jacuzzi watching cartoons on her big-screen TV.

One day the wife stood at the window overlooking the garden and thought to herself, "I really would like to plant some catnip for Katpunzel. I wish I had a garden."

Katpunzel had just walked into the room at that very moment. And having a very keen sixth sense, she could read people's minds. So she jumped up on the windowsill and smiled and said, "Catnip would be really nice—especially served on that silver platter you promised to buy me."

So later that night, when her husband got home, the wife asked him if he would help find the lady with the garden and ask if they could plant catnip. Because he loved her so much, and because she loved Katpunzel so much, he agreed. Besides, at least this wasn't going to show up on his Visa bill.

That evening, the couple took the elevator all the way down to the ground floor to try to find Garden Lady. Katpunzel, on the other hand, stayed in the condo and relaxed in her shiatsu chair while listening to Yanni on her new CD player.

At this point, you, the reader, may be getting the feeling that Katpunzel was really material-istic and lazy, that she should have been more thankful for her good fortune and less greedy. And you'd be right, but that doesn't change the facts.

Anyway, back down in the garden, the couple couldn't find Garden Lady, even though they called out, "Garden Lady, Garden Lady," over and over again. Finally, they went back upstairs.

But the wife insisted and Katpunzel agreed, they would just have to have some fresh catnip planted in that garden. So every day that week, on his way home from work, the husband stopped by the garden and called out, "Garden Lady, Garden Lady. Is there anyone here?" No one ever answered.

The weekend came, and the wife decided she would plant the catnip anyway. How could Garden Lady possibly object, she thought. She'd only plant a small patch over in the corner, out of the way.

So the wife left the condo on Sunday with a spade, a pair of gardening gloves, and a packet of catnip seeds. Katpunzel was eating a bagel and cream cheese and browsing through a Tiffany's catalog.

The wife had just finished planting her seeds and was wiping her hands on her pants when Garden Lady appeared as if by magic.

"What are you doing in my garden?" she yelled angrily.

The wife tried to explain about the catnip and Katpunzel and no children.

Garden Lady softened a little. "I didn't mean to yell, but this is my home. How would you like it if someone barged into your home without even knocking?"

"You mean you live here?" asked the wife. And just then she noticed a pile of blankets against the fence. "Is that where you sleep?"

"Yes," said Garden Lady proudly. "It's very peaceful here. And I love smelling my lavender when I'm drifting off to sleep."

Now here's a great example of where someone says one thing and the person hearing it
hears something else. While Garden Lady was
saying how much she enjoyed her home in the
garden, the wife heard this: "I don't have a
home. I'd love to come live with you in your
fancy condo up in the sky." Some people just
really don't know how to listen, do they?

Anyway, before Garden Lady knew what
had hit her, the wife had convinced her that
living in the garden was unsafe and unhealthy
and just not right. Especially when she, the
wife, had a beautiful condo that she would be
more than happy to share.

So, poof, as if by magic, the wife had talked
Garden Lady into staying in the spare bedroom with Katpunzel. She was sure Katpunzel
wouldn't mind sharing.

The wife was wrong. Katpunzel minded.

I mean, who wouldn't mind someone coming in and moving your stuff and changing the station on the radio and using your Jacuzzi?

Besides, Katpunzel didn't like the way Garden Lady looked. She had dirt under her fingernails. Her hair was unkempt. Her clothes were very much out of fashion. Let's face it, Katpunzel thought to herself, she clashes with the decor.

So every time Garden Lady came into the room, Katpunzel would hiss and arch her back. She was not a very good welcoming committee.

That night, as they were going to sleep (Katpunzel in the middle of the bed and Garden Lady hanging on to the edge by the corner of the sheet), Katpunzel heard Garden Lady crying softly.

At first this just annoyed Katpunzel because it was keeping her awake. But soon she started to feel sorry for the old lady. Katpunzel remembered her first night in the animal shelter and how she had cried herself to sleep.

"What's wrong?" meowed Katpunzel, half aggravated, half sympathetic.

"I can't sleep," said the woman. "I'm used to being out under the stars and feeling the night winds and smelling my beautiful lavender."

Katpunzel was perplexed. "But down there, you have nothing but the cold, hard ground to sleep on. Up here, there's this nice big bed, although it did seem bigger before you got here."

Garden Lady sobbed. "I don't need all this fancy stuff. I was perfectly happy in my garden."

Katpunzel was taken aback. Who wouldn't want a Jacuzzi and a shiatsu massage chair and a big-screen TV? "Well," she said finally, "why don't you just sneak out?" As she saw it, this would make both their lives better. Garden Lady could have her lavender, and Katpunzel could have the bed to herself.

"I don't want these nice people to think I'm ungrateful. And I do appreciate having three meals a day and a place to go to the bathroom. If only I could sneak out at night and sneak back in without anyone knowing."

"Well, you can," Katpunzel said cryptically. "I have an idea. You have to promise not to tell a soul."

"Okay," agreed Garden Lady.

"I will lower you out this window with my tail. And when you are ready to come back in, simply stand beneath this window and call up: 'Katpunzel, Katpunzel, let down your ebony tail,' and I will let you climb back up."

"Your tail is long and beautiful, but we're on the thirty-second floor," said Garden Lady.

"Ah, but you see, what no one knows is that I have a magic tail."

Garden Lady was dumbstruck. She wasn't sure about this whole magic tail business. And besides, she was a little scared of heights. But she really wanted to sleep in her garden. "What if it doesn't work?"

"Suit yourself," responded Katpunzel snippily. Boy, she had some mood swings.

"Okay, I'll try it," said Garden Lady.

So Garden Lady climbed out the window holding on to Katpunzel's tail. And just as she had promised, Katpunzel's tail grew longer and longer until, finally, Garden Lady was on the ground.

They both slept soundly.

Early the next morning, around 5:00 A.M.,

Katpunzel heard from below: "Katpunzel, Katpunzel, let down your ebony tail." She unfurled her long and beautiful tail, and it kept unfurling and unfurling until it reached all the way to the ground. Garden Lady climbed up.

They had Belgian waffles with real maple syrup for breakfast.

For almost a week, Katpunzel continued to let Garden Lady in and out of the condo on her tail. And, little by little, Katpunzel came to like Garden Lady.

Then one day, after hearing all those stories about the garden and its wonderful smells and the birds and the bees (no, not *those* birds and bees) and the butterflies, Katpunzel decided she had to see the garden for herself.

So Katpunzel and Garden Lady went out one day using the front door. After all, they couldn't very well sneak out; if Katpunzel was in the garden, how would they have gotten back in? She may have been a magical cat, but she wasn't that magical.

So Katpunzel saw the wonderful garden. And smelled it. And, of course, she visited nature. She could see why Garden Lady loved it here. It was beautiful. And that patch of catnip was especially nice.

While they were in the garden, Garden Lady made a decision: No more sneaking in and out to visit the garden. She would move back to her garden. It was the right place for her.

Katpunzel made a decision too.

She rode the elevator up to the thirty-second floor and pawed at the door. The wife opened it and let her back in.

Katpunzel hopped up on top of the microwave. She looked at the wife and said, "I want you to return all my stuff. The big-screen TV, the Jacuzzi, the jewelry. I don't need all that stuff."

The wife was shocked. "But I thought you liked that stuff."

"I thought I did too," replied Katpunzel. "But what I'd really like is if we took all the money and moved to the country where we can have our own garden. There I can watch the birds and the bees and the butterflies. And we can grow catnip."

The wife thought this was a great idea, so she discussed it with the husband that night.

And, through the magic of fairy tales, they sold all Katpunzel's stuff (except the shiatsu massage chair; you gotta have some luxuries); they sold their condo; they bought a house in the country; and they started their own garden.

And Garden Lady came to visit once a week to give them tips on making things grow.

And they all lived happily, and with green thumbs and paws, ever after.

Hope and a Prayer

A long time ago I found a long-haired gray cat with a white spot under her chin. She was the most beautiful creature I had ever seen. And when she purred, I could feel the whole room vibrate.

Even though my dad told me we couldn't have any animals in the house, I brought her home and hid her in the closet. I guess my dad figured that with seven kids, two adults, and more than our share of bugs, we had enough animals in the house. I figured that with the house that full, who would notice one little cat?

I named my new friend Hope. Because that's what I was doing. Hoping that I could keep her.

For three days, Hope was a secret from the rest of my family. I sneaked in food. I bought a cat box and hid it in my school backpack. I bit my tongue when Hope would play too rough and swat me good with her claws.

But on the fourth day, Hope meowed very loudly just as my dad was walking by, and the jig was up.

My dad yelled and he screamed and he stomped his feet about how he thought everyone understood that we just couldn't afford to have any animals in the house.

But I did what any little girl worth her salt would do. I cried. And, as it often does, it worked.

Besides, it probably didn't hurt that I told him that Hope was really good at catching cockroaches. So she would not be a pet, she would be an employee. I was something, wasn't I?

As I mentioned earlier, Hope was a beautiful cat. Apparently all the boy cats thought so too. Before long, they stood outside the windows begging and pleading for Hope to go on dates with them. It was pitiful. And believe me, I've seen human guys begging and pleading for dates (not with me, mind you, but on TV), and this was just as pitiful.

Being young and not knowing much about how these things work, I didn't worry much when Hope got out of the house one day. I figured she'd come back because all the good cockroaches lived in our house.

You can probably guess what happened next. No, she didn't run away and join the circus. No, she didn't become an Amway sales rep. No, not the old sprouted wings and flew to the moon thing. Come on, be serious. She got . . . you know . . . in a feline family way.

A few months later, she had kittens—seven of them. I guess she was trying to balance the cat-to-human ratio in the house.

They were beautiful kittens. Two were as black as velvet Elvis paintings (without the Elvis), four were gray like their mom (one with white socks), and one was white and gray and black and brown with a spot right on her eye. You could tell she was going to be trouble when she grew up. She would probably get her ears pierced and join a motorcycle gang.

You know that my dad had difficulty accepting one cat, so you can imagine how he felt about eight! He yelled and he screamed and he stomped. And I cried and I cried and I cried.

But this time it didn't work. That's the thing with crying; sometimes it works, sometimes it doesn't.

My dad said we would have to get Hope fixed. I cried because I thought that meant she was broken. And believe me, after delivering seven kittens, she looked like she might be broken.

So Hope went to the hospital, and I had to find people to adopt all her kittens. I made them fill out questionnaires; I ran credit checks; and I checked for criminal records. My babies were not going home with just anyone.

Hope spent the rest of her life being my friend and purring loud enough to vibrate the entire room. And catching cockroaches. She was happy. I was happy. And my dad eventually grew to love her too. I mean, who can resist a cat? You'd have to be made out of stone.

Sometimes, all these years later, I wonder about all those adopted kittens. I keep waiting for the Oprah show where they match up adopted cats looking for their birth mother's best friend. Hey, it could happen.

And I pray that those kittens are living healthy lives with loving people who don't wait until they are broken to have them fixed.

Alanis and Her Magic Belly

There was once a poor cat named Al. She lived on the street and ate out of trash cans. She was not a cat you'd ever see on *Catstyles of the Rich and Famous.*

Al had to work hard every day just to get enough food to live on. She was becoming depressed and downhearted. In Al's opinion, it was a cat-eat-cat world.

One gray, rainy day during the middle of a winter full of gray, rainy days, Al was running through the alley behind Mama Scarpachi's Fine Italian Food looking for pasta.

Al's coat was matted with the rain and mud, and she was not much to look at. The fact is, she'd given up grooming herself because, well, what was the point?

This was a low point in Al's life. And, to top it off, there was no pasta in the alley—only garlic bread. And Al was allergic to garlic. She ate it anyway because she was very hungry.

She sneezed all the way home. If you can call a small, wet spot under a big, wet rhododendron home.

Just as Al was slinking damply toward her bush, a young girl with bright blue eyes and beautiful red hair spotted her. "Mommy, look! A kitty! Can I take her home?"

The little girl, whose name was Susan, tugged on her mom's coat sleeve. Her mom took one look at Al, and it was all she could do to keep from blurting out, "That ugly thing? Heavens no. We'll get you a real cat from a pet store."

But Susan's mom didn't say that because Susan was adopted. And when Susan's mom had adopted her, Susan had been kind of scroungy-looking herself—not to mention wet, cold, and hungry.

So Susan's mom agreed that they could adopt the cat.

And before Al could say, "Excuse me, please, do I know you and by the way, you have really nice hair," Susan had scooped her up into her arms. She pulled Al into her coat, and they got in a nice, warm car.

Now, before you go thinking that Al had automatically landed in the lap of luxury, you should know that the car they got into was a 1974 Pinto.

But the heater worked. Al was startled and

surprised, but she was warm. And besides, she didn't know that a 1974 Pinto was really a lousy car.

The next day, Susan's mom took Al to the vet while Susan was at school, just to get checked out to see what needed to be done to nurse Al back to good health.

When the nurse asked what the cat's name was, Susan's mom said "Alanis," just like that. Al liked that—a lot. It showed that Susan's mom had taste. No matter what kind of car she drove.

The vet looked Al over and prescribed several nasty medicines. One was for worms, one was for runny eyes, one was for matted fur, and one was for . . . well, how can we put this delicately . . . gastrointestinal distress.

Susan's mom paid ten dollars and promised to pay the rest when she could afford it. She and the vet had gone to college together, so he trusted her to put the check in the mail, so to speak.

Then Susan's mom took Al home and washed her in the kitchen sink. You have to know that Al was not at all fond of this. And at first, she scratched and clawed and meowed and hissed. But Susan's mom kept talking to her in a calm voice and saying things like, "You're going to be so beautiful once we get finished, Alanis."

So Al decided to give in. This was not something she was used to doing.

Susan's mom dried her and combed out her hair. It was red with stripes. There was no way anyone would have known this, including Al, because she had spent her whole life covered with brown-gray mud.

Then Susan's mom massaged Al's ears. Al

really liked that. It almost made up for the bath, but not quite.

Finally, there she was. Alanis. A beautiful cat. A cat who could look at herself in the mirror and not run screeching in the other direction.

When Susan got home from school that afternoon, she hardly recognized Alanis. She dropped her books on the floor and got down on her knees and started to pet Alanis.

She petted her ears. She petted her back. She petted her chin.

Than she petted her belly. And when Susan petted Alanis's belly, something wonderful happened. Susan suddenly forgot about being called into the principal's office because the boy behind her had cheated off her test in math. She forgot about the girls who called her "Geek Girl" (Susan was, by the way, very,

very smart). She forgot about the fact that she hadn't been invited to the best birthday party of the year.

"Mom, come quick," Susan yelled.

Susan's mom came running over, expecting a problem. "What's the matter?" she asked.

"Nothing, Mom." Susan just smiled. "I think Alanis has a magic belly."

"What do you mean, magic?" Susan's mom asked suspiciously. "If I rub it will I get three wishes?" Susan's mom wasn't much for magic. You could understand—her life hadn't been too magic so far.

So Susan took her mom's hand and put it on Alanis's belly. Alanis was just in heaven with all this attention, *and* she smelled pasta cooking in the kitchen.

"Better than three wishes," Susan said. "Rub it."

Susan's mom began to rub Al's belly. Alanis began to purr. And what do you know, magic started to happen. Susan's mom no longer cared about tomorrow's deadline for that big report at the office. She forgot about that big argument she'd had with her best friend yesterday. And she wasn't even worried about not being able to afford the rent next month.

"You're right, this is magic!" Susan's mom exclaimed.

It must have been magic for Alanis too. Because pretty soon she forgot about the gray, rainy winter. She forgot about scrounging through trash cans for pitiful meals. She forgot about sleeping under the damp bush.

Alanis was happy because she was warm and beautiful and had fresh pasta (actually, it was Hamburger Helper, but Alanis didn't care). And she had catnip whenever she wanted it.

She also loved being a redhead. It went with her temperament.

Susan and her mom were happy because no matter what went wrong during the day, when they petted Alanis's belly their problems disappeared.

Now this is the best part of this fairy tale.

Alanis wasn't really a magic cat. The truth is that every cat has a magic belly. And if you rub it long enough, your problems will magically disappear.

Try it and see! It's magic.

Nursery
Rhymes

Cat Be Nimble

Cat be nimble
Cat be quick
Cat sit on the sofa and lick.

Little Ms. Kitty

Little Ms. Kitty
Was really quite witty
Amusing herself every day.
Along came a human
Who asked her to humor him
But suddenly she had nothing to say.

Row Your Boat

Row, row, row your boat gently down the stream
But leave your cat behind at home
He'd rather be on dry land drinking cream.

Humpty Kitty

Humpty Kitty sat on a wall
Humpty Kitty had a great fall
But because he was a feline supreme
He landed on his feet
and went on with his dream.

Little Cat Horner

Little Cat Horner
Sat in the corner
Eating her catnip pie
Stuck in her paw
And pulled out her ma
And said leave it alone, it's all mine.

This Little Kitty

This little kitty went to market
  *(where she munched on a fresh-caught tuna
  when no one was looking)*
This little kitty stayed home
  (and watched America's Funniest Cat Videos*)*
This little kitty had roast beef
  (not to mention potatoes and gravy)
This little kitty had none
  *(she was on a strict diet and spent dinnertime
  working out to* Felines of Steel*)*
And this little kitty went meow, meow, meow all
the way home
  *(because she was exhausted from a long day's
  work catching mice at the office. And when she
  finally got home, she had to turn off the TV,
  clean up the dinner dishes, put away the sweaty
  towels, and pick up after all the other kitties.
  Then she was exhausted and slept for twenty
  hours straight.)*